POEMS OF LIFE

By

Christine Gallant

Published by: Book Writing Pioneer

Cover design by: Book Writing Pioneer

ISBN: 979-8-9919076-2-0

Printed in: United States

Dedication

I dedicate this to all my friends and family for their support and encouragement.

CONTENTS

About the Author

I am from Greenfield Park, a little town south of Montreal, Quebec. I am 65 years old mother and grandmother. I have been retired for 10 years.

My passions are photography, travel and my newfound love of poetry.

I am from the old school, which was poems must rhyme. While taking a writing course online with Coach Janna Lopez, I was re-introduced to poetry with a new perspective.

Please sit back and enjoy!

Page Blank Intentionally

Introduction

Welcome to my first poetry book. It's in regard to everyday life. I have always wanted to write a book, but never thought it would be a Poetry book. With special encouragement from my writing coach, Janna Lopez, my dream is coming to fruition.

Take a seat and enjoy!!

Breathe

Breathe in, breathe out.

Feel the air going through your lungs.

Then take the plunge!!

Something you always wanted to do and never thought the time was right, but it's the time right now.

Once again, breathe in, breathe out.

You got this!!

C

Christmas carolers cheering on the children.

Clever coyotes clawing at the cow's carcass.

Chubby cubs clapping in the classroom.

Creeping caterpillar climbing up the Chevy Coupe.

Creole Queen

The Creole Queen, how grand you are...

Inviting your passengers aboard.

For an unforgettable journey down the Mississippi
River.

With roaring music and people dancing in the
moonlight.

Gazing back to the shore.

Their eyes light up from the dazzling beauty of
New Orleans at night.

Death

The love must go on

Even when you're gone.

The laughter and joy have been dimmed

But the fears and tears are still there.

Like the sand and the sea, we will meet again.

Detours

Life is like a city under construction everywhere
you look, there are detours.

Some are shorter than others.
Some take longer due to congestion
But in the end, they get us to where we need to be!!

Erase

Erase the place

Erase the face

Erase the time

Erase everything from your mind

And start all over again.

I Close My Eyes

I close my eyes

I see whales munching on dandelions and cheddar
cheese

I see buffalos dancing with miniature Chihuahuas

I see snakes swimming in a pot of hot chili

I see giraffes playing mini-golf

I see...

I hear leaves crunching below their feet

I hear an ambulance siren in the far distance. I
hear a doorbell ringing

I hear a dog barking as people scurry by
I hear...

I smell burnt toast

I smell freshly cut mint

I smell coffee brewing

I smell sweet apple pie

I smell...

Into The Night

Into the night, they go with strength and trepidation.

They had been through this many times before.

But this time, it felt different. But not in a good way.

There was howling in the distance.

The winds were picking up.

Were they really prepared for what was about to happen?

I don't think so!

Life

A Heartbeat is like a drum in a distant forest

A Breathe is like a whistle in the wind

A handshake is like a soft pillow on your cheek

Tears are like a river rushing downstream

Mother's Day

Mother's Day comes but once a year

But I'm your mother every day

I remember the day you were born.

I remember the day took your first steps.

I remember your first dance at your wedding.

I remember your first child being born.

Yes, I do because I'm your mother every day, not
just on Mother's Day.

When I am gone, will you
remember me every day,

or

Will you remember me just on Mother's Day?

Rain

It wasn't only rain.

There was a bolt of lightning.

There was thunder that was so deafening

It shook the ground under us as we lay in bed.

And as suddenly as it came.

It had all cleared up.

Ready, Aim, Fire

These three words together
are words of destruction.

Words you never want to hear together!!!
But alone, they bring a different meaning.

Ready

I'm ready to discover the world!!
Aim

Aim to get what you want in your future!!
Fire

There is a flicker of light at the end of the tunnel!!

Hopefully, one day, we never have to hear these
three words together again

S

The seasoned sailor on the inescapable seas

The silent sadness in my sister's eyes

The severed branch in the secluded forest

The sultry dancer swaying under the summer sky.

The silky body in the Steamy shower.

Scene

The scene was set,
everyone in their place.
But there was one element missing.

It was you.

You were always on time,
not even a hair out of place.

You looked stunning with a beautiful smile on your
face.

Where are you, my love?

The tree

So majestically standing before us.
You were so beautiful!

Shading us from the sun and purifying our air
around us.
Giving the insects food to feed off and squirrels to
play on.

Today, he chopped away at you ☹.

Life will never be the same

This Time

As they heard, the cavalry got closer

One by one, they climbed down the squeaky stairs under the floor.

They were safe there for now.

But for how long?

The doors swung open above them

The floors creaked as the soldiers searched the house.

Then there was silence.

They had finally left.

They were lucky this time!!

Today

Today was another day

Just like any other, so they say!

But wait a minute, it wasn't exactly like yesterday
There was a something different. You were not
there. But I could feel the wind on my hair.

Was it you letting me know everything was okay
as I continued walking, I saw a Blue Jay

I know you this was your favorite bird. You will
always be in my heart

And every day, I see a Blue Jay

I will know you are with me that day.

Doug Cote

1958-2022.